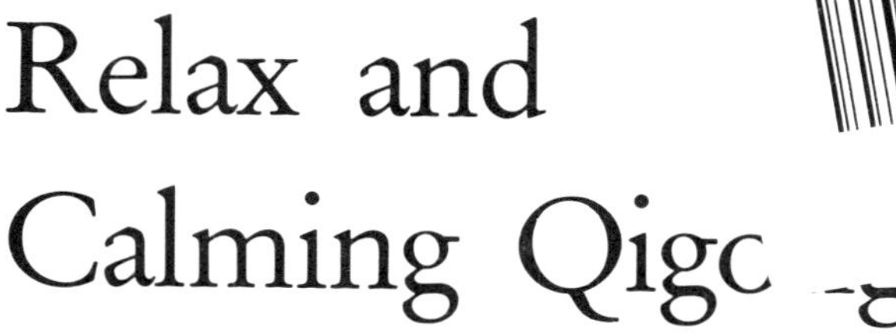

Relax and Calming Qigc g

Written by Wang Peisheng and Chen Guanhua
Translated by Chen Guanhua
English edited by Tony Rossi

HAI FENG PUBLISHING CO., LTD.
HONG KONG

Published by
Hai Feng Publishing Company
Rm. 1502 Wing On House
71 Des Voeux Rd., Central
Hong Kong

Printed by
Friendly Printing Co., Ltd.
Flat B1, 3/F., Luen Ming Hing Ind. Bldg.,
36 Muk Cheong St., Tokwawan
Kowloon, Hong Kong

First Edition November 1986
Second Edition November 1988
Third Edition June 1990
Fourth Edition April 1992
Fifth Edition July 1996

ISBN 962 238 181 2
HF-155-P
Published & Printed in Hong Kong

THE AUTHORS

Wang Peisheng, born in 1919 in Hebei Province, now lives in Beijing. At 13, Wang started to learn the Buddhist *Qigong* from his teacher, a nun named Miaochan Fashi in Jile'an, a Buddhist nunnery in Beijing. Wang Peisheng then studied the Taoist *Qigong* under an old Taoist Wang Zhenyi. In addition, he has been imbued in many other types of *Qigong*. Wang was also learning Confucian self-cultivation methods from Jin Hu and Xu Zhenkuan. At this time he learned *Taijiquan* and other forms of Chinese martial arts from various masters.

Since 1949, Wang Peisheng has been invited to teach *Taijiquan* and *Qigong* at such colleges and institutes as: Beijing Polytechnical Institute, Beijing Normal University, Beijing Normal College, Beijing Foreign Languages Institute, Beijing College of Mining Industry, the Central Drama College, Beijing College of Agriculture Mechanization, the Chinese Academy of Sciences and the Central College for Advanced Study of Sanitation. Wang's book *Wu Style Simplified Taijiquan* has been published in Chinese. Another book *Wu Style Taijiquan* has been published in English. The Chinese edition will be published soon.

Chen Guanhua, born in 1924 in Jiangxi Province, is 61 years old. He graduated in 1950 from the Department of Electrical Engineering of Qinghua University and in 1953 from the Beijing Russian Language Institute. He then worked as a scientific and technological Russian-Chinese interpreter for four years. Since 1956 Chen has been an engineer in the Ministry of Electric Power and its subordinate units. He is now a senior engineer of the Scientific and Technological Information Research Institute of the Ministry of Water Resources and Electric Power.

Chen began practising *Qigong* for several months in 1946. He once again began in 1963 and has practised *Qigong* continously since then. His master was Qin Zhengsan. Since

1981 Chen has been learning *Qigong* from Wang Peisheng.

Chen has published the following articles on *Qigong:* "The Key to *Qigong* Is Mastering your Mind" *Qigong Magazine,* No. 4, 1981;

"Making Three *Dantians* Linear" *Qigong Magazine* No. 2, 1982;

"Once Again About Making Three *Dantians* Linear" *Qigong Magazine* No. 1, 1983;

"Several Ideas on Spontaneously Moving *Qigong*" *Qigong Magazine and Science* No. 3, 1984;

"Qigong: Mastering the Mind" *China Daily,* Dec 31, 1984

Tony Rossi, born in 1948, graduated with a B.A. degree from the Geography Department and the Education Department of the Humboldt State University in Arcata, California, U.S.A. in 1974, and with an B.A. Degree from the History Department of the same university in 1977. Mr. Rossi taught history and geography in Australia for six years. He has been teaching English in China since 1980. He is now an English teacher at the Chinese Academy of Science.

While a student in the United States, he prastised Yoga for four years. Mr. Rossi has recently studied *Qigong*.

CONTENTS

INTRODUCTION

It is known that *qigong* is an effective means of curing diseases and improving health. In China, *qigong* has a 5,000-year history. As early as the Spring and Autumn and the Warring State Periods (770-221 B.C.), *qigong* had achieved high level of importance. Later Buddhism came to China and some of its features were added to *qigong*. During its several thousand years of progress, *qigong* has gained complexity and development. It is said that in China there are about 1,000 types of *qigong*, passed on by Taoist priests, Buddhist monks, Confucian scholars, *wushu* masters, doctors of traditional Chinese medicine, and others. Nowadays in China, Taoist *qigong* is becoming popular.

In Taoist opinion, the practice of *qigong* can be divided into five steps: Changing grain into semen, changing semen into *qi*, changing *qi* into spirit, returning spirit to nothingness, and combining nothingness with *tao*. The first step, changing grain into semen is the building foundation, in which the feeling of *qi* begins to appear and semen increases. When the change into *qi* is completed, *qi* can circulate along *ren-du* channels, i.e. along the middle lines of the chest, abdomen, back and head, which is called "small circulation." When the change of *qi* into spirit is completed, *qi* can circulate along all the main channels around the body, which is called "large circulation." For one who has completed the step returning spirit to nothingness, it is easy to enter the nothingness state, a higher-level *qigong* state, in which people feel their bodies are likely to disappear.

This book introduces two types of fundamental *qigong*, i.e. relaxing and calming *qigong* and shell *qigong*. It also introduces three other types of *qigong:* changing semen into *qi;* changing *qi* into spirit, and making three *dantians* (key acupoints) linear and experiencing the state of nihility.

These types of *qigong* are simple, easy to practice, and can quickly have positive effects in curing disease and improving health. People can make progress step by step in practicing these types of *qigong*. For young people, it usually takes one month to build the foundation, one hundred days to finish changing semen into *qi*, eighteen months to finish changing *qi* into spirit. For older persons or patients, more time is required. Ordinary people can achieve this, but only if they practice these types of *qigong* half an hour every day; *qigong* is no mystery.

WHAT IS QI?

The Chinese word *qi* (氣) usually means gas, as in air (*kongqi,* 空氣), or oxygen (*yangqi,* 氧氣). But sometimes *qi* has an extremely broad meaning. For example, in the famous poem *"Zhengqi Ge"* ("Song of Correct *Qi,*" 正氣歌), *Zhengqi* (correct or universal *qi,* 正氣) includes the sun, stars, mountains and rivers. According to the theory of traditional Chinese medicine, human life relies on *yuanqi* (original *qi,* 元氣). *Yuanqi* is translated into English as "original (inborn) vital energy."

What is the *qi* in *qigong?* It sometimes refers to the air we breathe, sometimes to the universal *qi,* or to the original vital energy (*yuanqi*). But there is also a special and important type of *qi,* which we can feel when practicing *qigong.* It is sometimes called "real *qi*" (*zhen qi,* 眞氣). After practicing *qigong* for a certain period of time, most people can feel that the acupoint on which their attention is concentrated becomes warm and expansive. This sensation is called "feeling of *qi.*" Along with a rise in your *qigong* level, a feeling of *qi* will develop. For example, after you successfully complete the step of changing semen into *qi,* the feeling of *qi* can circulate along the *ren-du* channels. After finishing the step of changing *qi* into spirit, your feeling of *qi* can circulate along all the main channels of the body. In other words, your feeling of *qi* will gradually develop and eventually be felt throughout your body. As a result, your original vital energy or *yuanqi* can be recovered, your chronic diseases cured, and your health improved. The feeling of *qi* may have some unknown connection with the air you breathe and the universal *qi.* It is known that the feeling of *qi* varies with the same frequency as breathing.

It is not known what causes the feeling of *qi.* Here we will introduce a hypothesis about it. In recent years some scientists have found that in the state of *qigong,* brain waves have a lower frequency and greater magnitude, and are more synchronized. Also, the temperature at the acupoint to which one's attention is directed is 1 to 3°C higher than other parts of the body. From modern physiology we know that such an action as bending a finger is caused by brain waves whose messages are sent to the finger through the nervous system; the terminal of the nerve releases some chemicals which enable the corresponding muscles to stretch or to retract. Proceeding from these facts, we propose that special brain waves, generated while practicing *qigong,* cause the expansion of the micrangium, thereby increasing the blood supply and stimulating the acupoint. Consequently there is a rise in temperature and other unusual phenomena at the acupoint, which in turn causes a feeling of warmth, expansion and other sensations – the feeling of *qi*.

As mentioned above, the feeling of *qi* depends on the mind; however, to a certain extent, it is independent of the mind. For example:

1. Even after having a short nap, one can maintain the feeling of *qi,* if one has felt it before the nap.

2. When calm, one can unconsciously reach the feeling of *qi* in some acupoints where he has previously concentrated his attention for a certain period of time and has therefore made it open to *qi*.

3. Sometimes one may experience the feeling of *qi* in "opened" acupoints, even though he may not be focusing his attention on those acupoints.

RELAXING AND CALMING QIGONG

This type of *qigong* can be practiced when one is standing, sitting, or lying down.

Body position:

a) Standing position (Fig. 1): Stand with feet shoulder-width apart and toes pointing forward, knees bent slightly, arms and hands naturally hanging down with palms facing legs, and eyes and mouth slightly closed.

b) Sitting position (Fig. 2): Sit erect on a stool with feet flat on the ground, legs shoulder-width apart, knees bent at a 90 degree, thighs perpendicular to the trunk, palms resting in a relaxed manner on thighs, shoulders down, chin slightly withdrawn, chest in, and eyes and mouth slightly closed.

Fig. 1 Standing position

Fig. 2 Sitting position

c) Lying position (Fig. 3): Lie flat on back with head on a pillow, arms laid comfortably by the sides of the trunk and palms facing downward, legs extended naturally, feet shoulder-width apart, toes pointing upward, and eyes and mouth slightly closed.

After adjusting your posture, concentrate your mind from the *baihui* acupoint through the *jianjing, shanzhong,* middle *dantian, huiyin, yinlingquan* and *sanyinjiao* acupoints, to the *yongquan* acupoint. After this, direct your mind to circulate the *qi* around the sole of your feet in the direction of your first toe to your little toe for one to three turns. Concentrating your mind on the *yongquan,* imagine that you are standing with each foot on the water of a small well, and that your *yongquan* is attached to the surface of the well water.

When your mind cannot concentrate on the *yongquan,* direct your thoughts along the outsides of your legs from the *yanglingquan* acupoint through the *huantiao, huiyin* and *mingmen* acupoints to the middle *dantian*. Then direct your mind to return to the *yongquan* in the way mentioned in the previous paragraph.

Relaxing and calming *qigong* can direct your turbid *qi* down to the ground and raise your clear *qi*. It may cure neurasthenia, tracheitis, hypertension, etc.

Fig.3 Lying position

SHELL *QIGONG*

Shell qigong is one of the basic types of *qigong,* simulating a shell with a mussel inside. It is devided into three stages.

First Stage: Raising the Mussel
This is the main stage of shell *qigong,* simulating a closed shell raising its mussel.

Body position:

Standing (Fig. 4): Stand with feet shoulder-width apart and toes pointing forward, with the knees bent slightly, shoulders relaxed and elbows down. Your arms hold your belly with your middle-finger tips attached to the sides of the navel. Close your eyes and mouth slightly.

Alternately keep your *laogong* and *shaohai* acupoints attached to your ***daimai*** (waistline channel). When you feel you have attached your *laogong* to your ***daimai***, you can direct your mind to attach your *shaohai* to your ***daimai***, and so on. The longer you practice, the better, but you shouldn't practice so long that you feel uncomfortable or tired. While you are

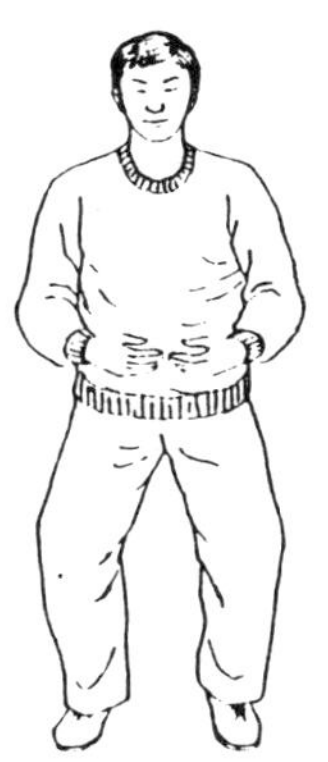

Fig.4

Fig.5

practicing this *qigong,* you can imagine that your arms hold a big ball, while your feet are on another big ball, and still another big ball is balanced on your head. Carefully make sure that the three big balls are aligned. When you feel the middle ball starting to wander, it is time to begin the second stage.

Second Stage: Opening the Shell
This state simulates opening a shell.

Procedure:
Slowly raise your arms to the level of your shoulder. Then you can imagine that your arms have touched the shell, but do not open the shell (Fig. 5). After a while, put your arms down and with the tips of your middle fingers massage the following acupoints: *qichong, yinlingquan, sanyinjiao, xuanzhong, yanlingquan,* and *huantiao.*

Then hold your hands on your back (Fig. 6 and Fig. 7). The tips of your middle fingers should point to the *mingmen* acupoint so that your two *laogong* acupoints and *mingmen*

Fig.6

Fig.7

form an equilateral triangle (Fig. 8). In figure (Fig. 8), the three acupoints are considered to be the centers of three circles. This is called "linking three rings with the moon".

Then bend backwards until you feel that the vertical triangle has become horizontal, like an opened shell. Stay in this position for a while until you feel that your *yongquan* acupoints have gone underground and your *baihui* acupoint has touched the earth. Then straighten your back, just as a bent bamboo naturally straightens after releasing stress. In this way the *baihui* acupoint will conduct the water of the *yongquan*★ upward. This is called "the head of a dragon conducts the water".

Relax your shoulders and place your hands by your sides. After taking a short break, you can begin the third stage.

Third Stage: Gathering the *Qi*

This stage simulates an open shell gathering food.

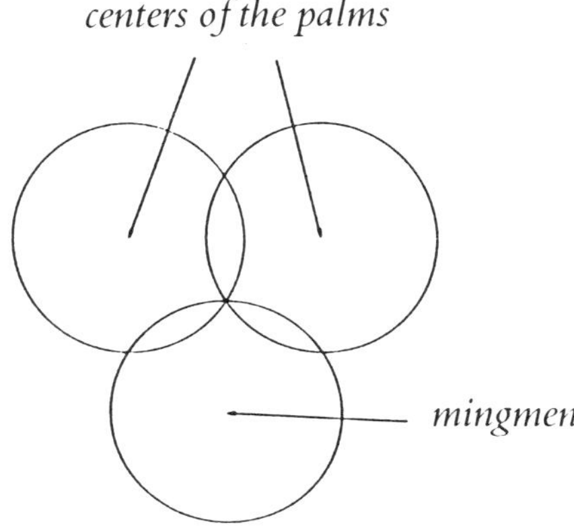

Fig. 8

★means a sprayed spring.

Procedure:
Raise your arms up, with the palms facing each other and with the elbows bent slightly, until the tips of your middle fingers reach eye level. The distance between tips of the two middle fingers should equal the distance between the centers of your eyes.

Touch your middle-finger tips together and then spread your hands apart, until the distance between the palms equals the width of your shoulders, as if from the middle-finger tip to the tip of the big toe, each side forms an opened shell. Touch your middle-finger tips together again, and then raise your hands, palms upward with your arms inclined to sides (Fig. 9). During this time your heels are raised. Then, while inhaling, concentrate your attention on the tip of your nose and imagine you are breathing *qi* from the sky into your lungs. Then lower your hands down in front of your eyes. Touch your middle-finger tips together. Then relax your shoulders and place your hands by your sides in front of your stomach (Fig. 10). During this time, concentrate your attention on the *renzhong* acupoint and imagine the real *qi* that you have just inhaled has come down to the middle *dantian*.

Fig.9

Fig.10

Repeat the above-mentioned sequence seven times.

Sunrise on the first, second, or third day of every lunar month is the best time to gather real *yin* from the sun. You can practice this third stage of shell *qigong* while facing the sunrise. You can get real *yang* from the rising moon when you practice this *qigong* on the 15th, 16th and the 17th of every lunar month.

Before completing the exercise, you should repeat for a short time the first stage of shell *qigong*.

By practicing shell *qigong*, you can achieve the same results that are possible with relaxing and calming *qigong* and the type of *qigong* called "making three *dantians* linear", which will be discussed later.

CHANGING SEMEN INTO *QI*

Semen is a treasure of the human body. You should not release semen too often. One who has changed semen into *qi* can feel happy and brisk and can cure diseases and improve his health.

People can begin to practice this method of *qigong* only when they have achieved a certain level of *qigong,* that is, they have practiced foundation-building *qigong* such as relaxing and calming *qigong* or shell *qigong*, and have achieved enough *yangqi* (positive qi).

How is it possible to know when one has enough *yangqi?* There are three indications: the first is if one has enough semen; the second is if his genital organ becomes hard more often than before; and the third is when one has felt that enough *qi* has circulated along his waistline channel. According to these indications, one can know whether he can begin practicing changing semen into *qi*.

Procedure:

1. After three respirations, with your mind concentrated on your throat, shift your attention alternately to the navel and the *mingmen* acupoint – to the navel when exhaling, to the *mingmen* when inhaling. Keep breathing naturally throughout this time.

After some period of time you will feel, when exhaling, *qi* going from the middle *dantian* (behind the navel) through the *huiyin* to the *yongquan*. When inhaling, you will feel *qi* coming from the *yongquan* through the *huiyin* to the *mingmen*. During this time, one of the three key acupoints in the back, *changqiang,* is open to *qi*.

2. Having achieved this, you can try to open the other two key back acupoints: *jiaji* and *yuzhen*. To open the *jiaji:* while exhaling, concentrate your attention on the navel; while inhaling, concentrate on the *jiaji*. After a period of time you will have the feeling of *qi* in your *jiaji*. You will feel as though your *jiaji* is warm and expanded. Then you will feel *qi* passing

from your *mingmen* to your *jiaji,* and this feeling will get progressively stronger. If the width of this feeling is equal to the width of your palm, your *jiaji* is open to *qi*. Then you can use the same method to open your *yuzhen,* i.e., concentrate attention on your navel while exhaling, and guide your mind from the *mingmen* through the *jiaji* to the *yuzhen* while inhaling. When the midth of the feeling of *qi* at *yuzhen* reaches the width of the palm, your *yuzhen* is open to *qi*.

3. After the three key back acupoints have been opened to *qi* and *qi* has gone to the *yuzhen,* you should imagine that you are looking upward and backward, then look forward in order to direct your *qi* to the *baihui* acupoint. After being there for a while, *qi* will automatically go forward and stay at the place between *baihui* and *naomen**. Then you will feel that the top of your head is warm and clear and that your whole body is very comfortable. You should keep this feeling as long as possible and eliminate any distractions.

4. When you cannot keep *qi* at the top of your head, *qi* will automatically go down to the middle *dantian.* During this movement you should not guide *qi* but just let it go. This is important because otherwise *qi* may go the wrong way or stop somewhere. *Qi* usually moves down in three ways: along the nose and eyes, collecting at the *renzhong* acupoint. At that time you should keep your tongue flat and the *qi* will move down. The *ren-du* channels will be connected and then *qi* will move down along the *ren* channel or *chong* channel to the middle *dantian*. At that time you would have finished one small circulation.

5. Using the above-mentioned methods, continue the circulation. It is usually better not to make more than nine small circulations at one time.

Before stopping you should concentrate your *qi* in the middle *dantian*.

Points to remember:

You can practice the changing semen into *qi* type of *qigong* while standing, sitting or lying down. When lying down, you should use a higher pillow and not let the *qi* stay at the top of your head.

While practicing, you should eliminate any distractions but don't be nervous. When the *qi* has reached the top of your head, you should not concentrate your mind on the place where the *qi* is, otherwise you will develop a condition referred to as "fire"★★. At that time you should only maintain the special, comfortable feeling. While you should not forget *qi,* you should also not help it move; simply allow the *qi* to progress naturally.

Usually it will take one hundred days to finish the entire process of changing semen into *qi*. You should progress gradually and steadily. You should not go on to the next step until the previous step has been mastered. In this way you can gain the benefits and will avoid any mistakes.

★ corresponds to the soft spot on an infant's head.

★★ "fire" is a illness with symptoms of heat such as constipation, inflammation of the nose and oral cavity, conjunctival congestion, etc.

CHANGING *QI* INTO SPIRIT

After completing the step of changing semen into *qi,* you can begin to practice changing *qi* into spirit. When you finish this step, your *qi* will pass through all the main channels of the body. Wherever your mind is concentrated, the feeling of *qi* will be there. You will feel brisk, clear-headed, and your diseases may be alleviated or cured.

Procedure:

1. Turn your tongue around three times in your mouth. Then your saliva will increase. When you swallow the saliva, your mind should follow it and conduct the *qi* to your pubic bones.

2. After attaining the feeling of *qi* in your pubic bones, you should shift your attention to the tips of your big toes.

3. After the feeling of *qi* comes into your big toes, you should relax them and shift your attention to your heels, and so on. Subsequently, shift your attention to following acupoints: *weizhong, huantiao* and *huiyin.*

4. After *qi* goes from *huiyin* through your anus to *changqiang,* shift your attention to the *jiaji* acupoint.

5. After getting the feeling of *qi* at the *jiaji* acupoint, you should shift your attention to the *jiquan* acupoint in the armpits, then to the *zhongchong* acupoints at the tips of the middle fingers, then to the *jianjing* acupoint and back to the *jiaji* acupoint.

6. Then shift your attention to your *yuzhen* acupoint. After getting *qi* to the *yuzhen* acupoint, you should shift your attention to the back of your ears and circulate *qi* around your ears one to three times, then back to the *yuzhen* acupoint.

7. When you feel enough qi at the *yuzhen* acupoint, you should imagine that you are looking upward and backward, then look forward in order to direct your *qi* to the *baihui*

acupoint. *Qi* does not stop at the top of your head but goes down through your face to the *renzhong* acupoint, then through your tongue to the *ren* channel. At that time you should have finished one large circulation.

8. Turn your tongue around three times after every three large circulations. All together, nine large circulations should be done; therefore this *qigong* is also called *Jiu Zhuan Huan Hun Dan* ("nine circulations to recover your spirit").

9. Before stopping, direct your *qi* back to the middle *dantian*.

Points to remember:

1. You can practice this *qigong* while standing, sitting or lying down. The body positions are the same as in practicing the relaxing and calming type of *qigong*.

2. Don't pay atttention to your breathing, and close your eyes naturally.

3. Don't be in a hurry to shift to the next acupoint until you have achieved the feeling of *qi* at the acupoint where you are.

4. Beginners should only pay attention to the acupoints, and not the channels. After you practice this type of *qigong* for some period of time, your channels will be automatically open to *qi*.

5. Don't pay attention to any images or other extraordinary phenomena, if they appear.

6. If you are frightened when practicing *qigong,* you should massage the last joints of your ring fingers with the tip of your thumbs and massage the two sides of your arms with your palms.

7. After finishing the process of changing *qi* into spirit, you can conduct the *qi* to the place where you have felt some pain from a disease. This may help cure the disease.

8. While practicing *qigong,* you may happen to reach a state in which you feel that your own body is likely to disappear and you have attained a special, comfortable feeling. That means you are in the nothingness state. In other words, you have changed spirit back to nothingness. You should maintain such a state as long as possible.

SOME EXPERIENCES IN THE NOTHINGNESS STATE

Entering the nothingness state is the goal of most of the higher-level types of *qigong,* passed on by Taoist priests, Buddhist monks, Confucian scholars, *wushu* masters, doctors of traditional Chinese medicine, and others. In short, all the schools of *qigong* lead to nothingness.

The phenomena and feeling of nothingness are different for different persons and at different times.

The nothingness state or state of nihility is very helpful for curing diseases and promoting health. Before entering nihility in order to cure a disease, one should conduct the *qi* to the point of pain; while in the state of nihility, the symptoms of the disease appear automatically, and the pain caused by the disease is almost the same as when the disease is active or present. After the appearence of pain, you can concentrate your attention on the point of pain for five to ten minutes. Then the disease will be alleviated. New and minor disease, such as a light cold, can be cured after only one treatment.

How can one enter nihility?

1. By practicing *qigong* in a quiet place and in a calm and relaxed state.

2. Letting the *qi* follow the large circulation step, i.e. he enters a state in which he has achieved the feeling of *qi* all over his body.

3. By thinking of nothing, not even about entering nihility. He keeps in mind the Chinese proverb: "All are false in the state with a wish, it is true only in the state without any wish".

Some people can enter nothingness more easily while lying down than when standing. Such a person should recall the feeling of nihility when he practices *qigong* in a standing position.

What phenomena are there in nihility?

1. While one is entering the state of nothingness, a white light with a colored spot the size of a button will usually appear in front of the eyes. The white light and the colored spot will disappear after he has entered the state of nihility.

2. He will feel that his body is likely to disappear.

3. His self-regulating ability will be improved so that he can prolong the duration of *qigong* and feel very comfortable.

4. The resistance of his skin to electricity may be remarkably reduced.

In addition, there is another phenomenon that merits mention: one person practiced *qigong* in a standing position for a long period but then, in order to enter the state of nothingness more easily, he changed to practicing *qigong* in a lying position. As a result, the strength of his legs was reduced. Later, he practiced *qigong* in both standing and lying positions and the strength in his legs became as great as before. This example shows that we should combine the ways of entering into the state of nothingness with other physical training so as to improve both "spirit and physical power".

MAKING THREE *DANTIANS* LINEAR

This type of *qigong* has been passed on by a Taoist priest by the name of Wang Zhenyi. While practicing this type of *qigong* you should concentrate your attention on making the upper, middle and lower *dantians* linear. When you have made your three *dantians* linear, you will attain a very special and comfortable feeling and will almost forget everything. Your small and large circulations will automatically be open to *qi*. This type of *qigong* can help you to recover quickly from fatigue. No matter how tired you are, you can completely recover after practicing this *qigong* for fifteen minutes. You can do this type of *qigong* while standing, sitting, lying down, or when practicing *taijiquan* or riding a bicycle. This *qigong* does not require any preparation or special procedure before stopping.

Procedure:

1. Soon after concentrating your mind in your upper *dantian,* shift your attention to the lower *dantian* (*huiyin* acupoint).

2. After getting the feeling of *qi* in the lower *dantian,* shift your mind to the middle *dantian* and arrange it in line with the upper and lower *dantians* in order to make the three *dantians* linear. Then imagine the three *dantians* as three spheres. You should carefully put the sphere of the middle *dantian* between the two spheres of upper and lower *dantians*. The middle sphere will slide out if you do it carelessly.

3. When the three *dantians* have been made linear, you will get a very special and comfortable feeling. You should hold this feeling as long as possible. It can help you return to the "original state", to cure diseases and promote your health. You should maintain this feeling and eliminate any distractions.

ESSENTIAL POINTS TO REMEMBER

1. Faith, resolve and perseveranc are three important factors for successful *qigong*.
2. One should keep still and be relaxed when practicing *qigong*.
3. Be natural and follow the natural law. Ignore the various reactions which may occur while practicing *qigong* – don't be afraid of them and don't be interested in them either. In brief, don't hope to achieve quick results, but concentrate on making no mistakes.
4. Beginners should concentrate their attention on the palms of their hands and the soles of their feet.
5. Beginners should pay no attention to their breathing, but breathe naturally.
6. Don't guide your *qi* to your head too early or too often. Otherwise, you may suffer from excessive internal heat (with such symptoms as constipation, conjunctivities and inflammation of the nose and oral cavities). For patients suffering from such diseases as hemicrania, it is necessary to guide their *qi* to the head. In this case they should pay some attention to the *yongquan* and *mingmen* acupoints to reduce excessive heat.

   The saliva under your tongue will be continuously produced, if you practice *qigong* in the correct manner. You will suffer from xerostomia if you have excessive internal heat. Sometimes you may suffer from xerostomia when your attention is concentrated on your *yongquan* acupoint too often. In this case, you should pay some attention to the *mingmen* acupoint in order to conduct the "water" of your *yongquan* up to your head.

   Mastering the duration and degree of internal heat (which is connected with the mind) is an important problem when practicing *qigong*.

7. For some types of *qigong*, such as relaxing and calming *qigong* and the first stage of shell *qigong*, the longer you practice, the better. But do not hurry. You should gradually increase the duration of practice. You should feel comfortable and not be tired after each session. In practicing *qigong*, if you suffer from xerostomia and there isn't too much distractive thought, the xerostomia may be caused by inappropriately long duration of practice. In that case, shorten the practice.
8. Semen is one of the treasures of the human body; don't release it too often. When you feel that the semen will be released, you can guide it from the male genital organ to the *huiyin* acupoint; then guide it along the spine to the head. This is called "changing semen into *qi*".
9. Every time before stopping practice, direct the *qi* back to the middle *dantian*.
10. Do some suitable massage after practising *qigong* (see *Traditional Chinese Fitness Exercises*, published by New World Press, Beijing, 1984).

Appendix I:

QIGONG: MASTERING THE MIND*

The translation of *qigong* as "a system of breathing exercises" (*China Daily*, October 19, 1984) may create misunderstanding among foreigners.

I have been practicing *qigong* for more than 20 years. *Qigong* is good for health and longevity. It cured me of many diseases, such as: lipomatosis in hepar, arthritis, rhinitis, gastroenteritis and hemicrania. I have learned more than ten types of *qigong*. In doing most of them we needn't pay attention to breathing, but keep breathing naturally. A few types of *qigong* require the regulation of breath, but mastering your mind is still the key. For this reason I have written an article, entitled "The key to *qigong* is mastering your mind," which was published in *Qigong* magazine No. 4, 1981.

It is said that in China there are about 1,000 types of *qigong*, passed on by Taoist masters, Buddhists, Confucians scholars, *wushu* masters, doctors of traditional Chinese medicine, and others. Among so many types of *qigong* there are some points in common. The common points for most types of *qigong*, I think, are stillness, relaxation, and a sort of naturalness. Stillness means thinking nothing, except the essentials of practicing *qigong*. Relaxation means keeping the mind and muscles relaxed. "To be natural" means one should follow the natural law and not be nervous.

For most types of higher-level *qigong*, there is another common point, entering the state of nihility. In such a state, people feel their bodies are likely to disappear. Entering the nihility is very helpful for health and longevity. In all the common points mentioned above, mastering the mind is the most important. The regulation of breathing is of secondary importance. Therefore, the key to *qigong* is not the breathing exercise.

Beijing Chen Guanhua

* This article was published in *China Daily,* December 31, 1984.

Appendix II.

DIAGRAM OF RELEVANT ACUPOINTS

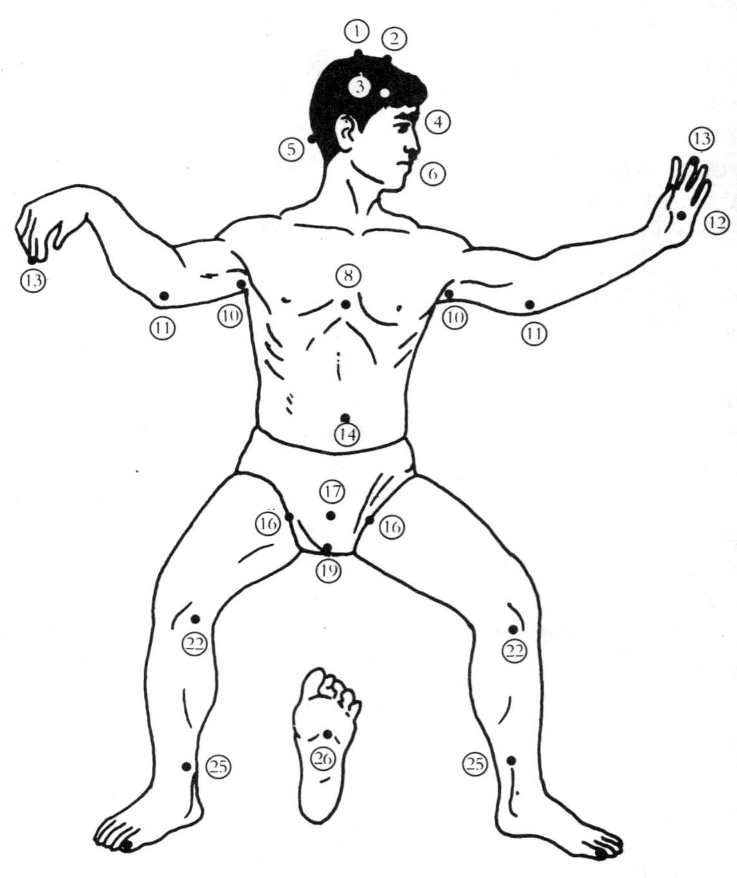

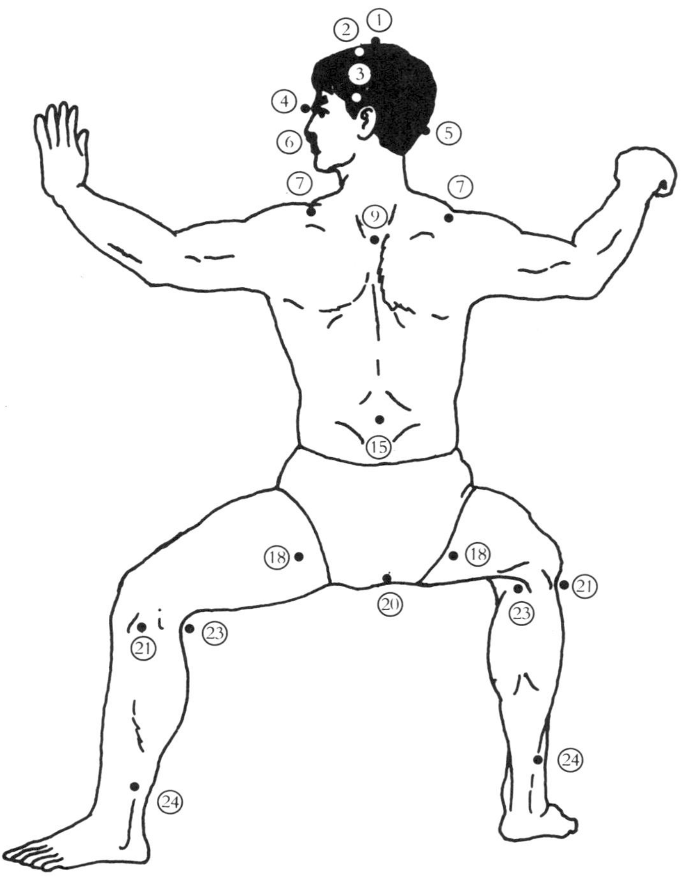

1. *Baihui* 2. *Naomen* 3. Upper *dantian* 4. *Xuanguan* 5. *Yuzhen*
6. *Renzhong* 7. *Jianjing* 8. *Shanzhong* 9. *Jiaji* 10. *Jiquan* 11. *Shaohai*
12. *Laogong* 13. *Zhongchong* 14. Middle *dantian* 15. *Mingmen*
16. *Qichong* 17. Pubic bones 18. *Huantiao* 19. Lower *dantian* (*Huiyin*)
20. *Changqiang* 21. *Yanglingquan* 22. *Yinlingquan* 23. *Weizhong*
24. *Xuanzhong* 25. *Sanyinjiao* 26. *Yongquan*

Appendix III:

LOCATION OF RELEVANT ACUPOINTS

No.	Name	Location
1	*Baihui*	On the top of the head.
2	*Naomen*	Corresponds to the soft spot on an infant's head.
3	Upper *dantian*	A region in the frontal part of the brain one inch behind the *xuanguan* acupoint (between eyebrows) and one inch under the *naomen*.
4	*Xuanguan*	In the middle between two eyebrows.
5	*Yuzhen*	In the pit just below occipital bone. About one inch above the back hairline in the middle of the back of the head.
6	*Renzhong*	In the middle of the groove under the nose and above the lip.
7	*Jianjin*	On the shoulder about two inches from the neck. Under the tip of your middle fingers, while you cross hands on either side of the neck with thumbs next to the neck.
8	*Shanzhong*	In the pit of the stomach.
9	*Jiaji*	Three inches below the greater cervical vertebra.
10	*Jiquan*	In the armpit.
11	*Shaohai*	At the inside end of the transverse line across the elbow joint, when the elbow is bent.

No.	Name	Location
12	*Laogong*	In the centers of palms.
13	*Zhongchong*	In the tip of the middle (second) finger.
14	Middle *Dantian*	Behind the navel, three-tenths of the distance between the navel and the *mingmen* acupoint on the back.
15	*Mingmen*	Located on the back and opposite to the navel.
16	*Qichong*	Mid-way from the crotch to the hip. In the transverse line across the hip joint (about 1 inch lower than the middle point of the transverse line).
17	Pubic bones	
18	*Huantiao*	In the pit behind the greater trochanter of the femur. In the side of your buttock.
19	Lower *Dantian*	i.e. *huiyin* acupoint (perineum). It is located in the middle point between the genitalia and anus.
20	*Changqiang*	A half an inch below the lower end of the coccyx.
21	*Yanglingquan*	In the pit before and beneath the upper condyle of the calf bone, while the knee is bent. About two inches below the knee and in the middle of the outside of the leg.

No.	Name	Location
22	*Yinlingquan*	In the pit behind and beneath the upper end of the tibia, when the knee is bent. About two inches below the knee and in the middle of the inside of the leg.
23	*Weizhong*	In the center of popliteal space at the back of the knee.
24	*Xuanzhong*	Three inches above the outside ankle-joint and behind the calf bone.
25	*Sanyinjiao*	Three inches above the inside ankle-joint and behind the tibia.
26	*Yongquan*	In the pit of the front part of the sole while toes are crimped.

Note: One inch equals the distance between two transverse lines of the middle section of your middle finger.

Appendix IV:

EXAMPLES OF CURING DISEASES AND EXPERIENCES IN PRACTISING SPECIFIC TYPES OF *QIGONG*

A. An Example of Curing Fatty Liver

The subject: Chen Guanhua, male, 61 years old, senior engineer of the Scientific and Technological Information Research Institute of the Ministry of Water Resources and Electric Power.

In 1981, before he practiced the types of *qigong* described in the preceding pages, although he had been practicing *qigong* for more than ten years, his small circulation hadn't been fully open to *qi*. He rarely tried to open his large circulation to *qi*. In 1981, after he practiced these types of *qigong* for a short period of time, his small and large circulation became fully opened to *qi*; furthermore, he can enter the nihility state quite often while practicing *qigong*. Along with the rise in his *qigong* level, his health has become remarkably better. A pain in his liver had lasted for more than 20 years. In 1980 the results of ultrasonic examinations showed that he suffered from fatty liver (lipomatosis in hepar). This disease could not be cured by either western or traditional Chinese medicine. It was cured by practicing these types of *qigong*. In 1984 an ultrasonic examination showed that the symptoms of fatty liver had disappeared and the pain in his liver has also disappeared. From 1980 to 1984, he did not use any measures other than *qigong* to cure his fatty liver condition.

While practicing these types of *qigong*, it is difficult for people to make mistakes; moreover, in different situations they can adjust the procedure to correct any errors. For example, in the past while practicing *qigong*, Mr. Chen had too often concentrated his attention on the top of his head; therefore, he often had excessive internal heat and as a result his sight was often impaired. His hair also had become prematurely white. Since he has practiced these types of *qigong*, the symptoms of excessive internal heat and impaired sight, have been alleviated and his health has also remarkably improved. In addition, these types of *qigong* require the regulation of the mind but not the regulation of breath. In the past when Mr. Chen practiced a type of breath-control *qigong*, he sometimes suffered from a pain in his chest and the side of his body. While practicing the types of *qigong* described in this book he has avoided such mistakes.

In addition, for each step of these types of *qigong*, from foundation-building to changing spirit back to nothingness, there are certain indications and phenomena by which one can know whether or not to begin the next step. This can help people who practice *qigong* to progress steadily, step by step.

B. An Example of Eliminating Fatigue by Practicing "Making Three *Dantians* Linear" *Qigong*.

The subject: Zhang Zhankui, works in the Chunjian Primary School, Luohan Township, Huangpi County, Hubei Province.

After practicing "Making Three *Dantians* Linear" *Qigong*, Mr. Zhang summarized the advantages of this type of *qigong* as follows:

1. ***It is easy to enter a meditative state.*** In practicing some other types of *qigong* people concentrate their attention only on one part of the body, which is rather boring, and it is difficult to meditate. While practicing "Making Three *Dantians* Linear" *Qigong*, people should concentrate their attention on upper, middle, and lower *dantians* and should make the three *dantians* linear. This more complicated procedure makes it easier to meditate. Such *qigong* can help *qi* and blood circulate regularly and not wander, which in turn is helpful in avoiding mistakes. Besides, this type of *qigong* can open the channels of the body to *qi* and can help people relax and eliminate distractions. In short, it can help people enter the special state of *qigong*.

2. ***It can save time.*** In the past Mr. Zhang practiced *taiji qigong* three times a day, which took him about two hours every day. In addition, the procedures of *taiji qigong* are very complicated and require a quiet environment. He was often frightened while practicing *taiji qigong* in an unsuitable environment.

"Making Three *Dantians* Linear" *Qigong* doesn't require any special preparation or procedure for stopping. Therefore, it takes a short time to practice. Since he is familiar with this type of *qigong*, it usually takes him about 15 minutes to enter the state of *qigong*. Besides it does not have any side effects, even if another person interferes with him while he is practicing.

3. ***The effect is remarkable.*** In practicing "Making Three *Dantians* Linear" *Qigong* he can quickly enter the *qigong* state and therefore achieve quick results in curing diseases and promoting health. During practice, the saliva in his mouth is continuously produced. After practice he has a good appetite, sleeps well, and is full of vigor. In the past, if he worked until midnight, he would feel tired the next day. Now he can work until midnight, even to dawn, without being tired if he practices this type of *qigong* for 15–30 minutes after work. He can enjoy same benefits by practicing this *qigong* even after he has done heavy manual labor. For example, during the busy farm seasons, when he has done heavy manual labour for more than ten hours a day, he can quickly recover from being tired after practicing this type of *qigong*.

(from *Qigong* magazine No. 5, 1983)

C. An Example of Preventing and Correcting an Error by Practising "Making Three *Dantians* Linear" *Qigong.*

The subject: Su Wu, works in Guandu Middle School, Zhushan County, Hubei Province.

Mr. Su has practiced Hongshashou (a type of hard

qigong) for about one year; now his *qi* can reach the palms and fingers of his hands and his hands are very strong. But at times it was difficult for him to meditate and his *qi* wandered around in his abdomen. He couldn't solve this problem even when he applied some different methods to guide the *qi*. Since Mr. Su has studied "Making Three *Dantians* Linear" *Qigong*, he practices it from five to ten minutes before he practices Hongshashou. After three days of practice the problem of wandering *qi* was solved. Meanwhile, he found that "Making Three *Dantians* Linear" *Qigong* not only can prevent and correct errors, but can also help him to meditate, to relax his whole body, and it has cured him of insomnia.

(from *Qigong* magazine No. 2, 1984)

D. An Example of Curing Hysteria, Gastritis, and Coronary Heart Disease

The subject: Wen Shenglan, female, 48 years old, works in the Ministry of Geology and Mineral Products.

For several years before 1966, she suffered from pain in her whole body, the cause of which was unknown. In March 1966 the symptoms became serious. She constantly cried and her moods changed suddenly. According to the diagnosis of Third Hospital of the Beijing Medicine Institute, she suffered from hysteria. A long period of treatment, using both western and traditional Chinese medicine methods, had failed to cure her. In addition, she suffered from coronary heart disease and gastritis. Her blood pressure was very high and heart-stroke occured very often. Several times she was critically ill and was sent to the hospital for emergency treatment. Sometimes she would suddenly faint and have a weak pulse. At times she suffered from frequent irregular systole and was often extremely weak. Even in the summer time she had to wear heavy cotton-padded trousers, two pairs of woollen pajamas and cotton-padded shoes to keep warm. People were not permitted to use fans when Wen Shenglan was in a room. She could not fan herself because her bones would ache. When she was frightened a little, her legs would feel loose and she could not walk at all.

Since 1982, Wen has been practicing the types of *qigong* and the 37-postures *taijiquan*, taught by Wang Peisheng (see *"Wu-Style Taijiquan"* by Wang Peisheng and Zeng Weiqi). Her diseases have been gradually alleviated and her health has recovered. Hysteria has been cured, her heart stroke has not occured for a long time, and gastritis, from which she suffered for 40 years, has also been cured. Meanwhile practicing these types of *qigong* and *taijiquan* has cured her of some other diseases such as arthritis, pelvic inflammation, heavy constipation, and abdominal distention. Now she has become healthy and in the summer she doesn't have to wear winter clothing; moreover, she can fan herself when necessary. She said, "In the past, I was a person who suffered from serious diseases. *Qigong* and *taijiquan* have rescued me from the hands of the King of Hell."

E. An Example of Curing Hypertension, Nephritis, and Piles

The subject: Xu Wenming, male, 60 years old, driver for the Beijing Trolleybus Company.

In the past Mr. Xu suffered from several diseases, including hypertension, nephritis, and piles. His blood pressure was 190/120 mm. The results of his urine test were: urinary albumin++, white blood cells 0.3–0.5, red blood cells 0.5–1.0. He did not recover after his piles had been treated; a swelling in his anus appeared, when he suffered from excessive internal heat.

Since June 1983, Mr. Xu has been practicing *qigong* and 37-postures *taijiquan*, taught by Wang Peisheng. He practices for an hour and a half each morning, and has achieved remarkable results. His blood pressure has now been reduced to 150/100 mm. Tests have also revealed that the symptoms of his nephritis have been remarkably alleviated. The results of a urine test: urinary albumin reduced to +, white blood cells – 0.1, red blood cells – 0.3. His piles and splenopathy have been completely cured. He now eats and sleeps very well and has become a brisk walker. He can work for a long time without being tired. He has not needed to see a doctor for more than one year. His temper has become better.

F. An Example of Curing Hepatitis

The subject: Zhang Xixiu, male, 50 years old, employed in the Beijing Nuclear Instrument Factory.

In 1983 Mr. Zhang suffered from hepatitis. His transaminase was as high as 495 (in a healthy person, the transaminase is less than 160). At that time, in addition to resting and taking some medicine to protect his liver, he practiced the relaxing and calming *qigong* and 37-postures *taijiquan*. While practicing, he usually concentrated his attention on the tip of the third finger. After one-month of practice he went to the hospital for a follow-up examination and found that his transaminase had been reduced to 66 and the other indicators of liver function were all at normal levels. The doctor was surprised and said, "You have been cured quite quickly!"

G. An Example of Curing Coronary Heart Disease and Constipation

The subject: Zhang Shuyun, female, 61 years old, a cadre of Beijing Foreign Language Institute.

Zhang suffered from coronary heart disease with heart strokes and irregular systole. She also suffered from constipation. Since 1981 she has been practicing these types of *qigong* and 37-postures *taijiquan*. The symptoms of the diseases have gradually alleviated. There has been no recurrence of heart stroke or irregular systole. She no longer suffers from constipation.

H. An Example of Curing Amnesic Syndrome and Puffiness

The subject: Peng Wenzhang, male, 53 years old, a secretary in Secretariat of the General Office of the Ministry of Geology and Mineral Products.

Mr. Peng suffered from a amnesic syndrome. As a secretary he was to keep the minutes of meetings, but he could not remember the names of those attending; therefore, he was unable to fulfil his main task. Besides, he could not read documents, did not sleep well, and often lost his temper, which had not been characteristic of him.

Since early 1984 Mr. Peng has been practicing *qigong* and 37-postures *taijiquan*, taught by Wang Peisheng, and has achieved remarkable curative results. Now Mr. Peng eats and sleeps well and his memory functions well. He can now keep the minutes of a meeting, read documents, and even write articles. Meanwhile, the symptoms of puffiness, which he had suffered from, also disappeared. He has become a brisk walker, and a healthy strong man.

I. An Example of Recovering One's Youthful Vigor

The subject: Xie Shanchu, male, 74 years old. He was a businessman in Beijing and now lives at 30 Dong Yang Ma Ying Street, Western District, Beijing.

Mr. Xie was very weak and walked in a doddering manner. Since 1983 he has been practicing *qigong* and 37-postures *taijiquan*, taught by Wang Peisheng, now Mr. Xie has recovered his youthful vigor and walks like a young man.

目錄

作者簡歷

一. 王培生：1919年生於河北省，現居北京。13歲時，曾拜北京極樂庵妙禪法師爲師，受過居士戒（法號印成），學過佛教氣功；後又向老道士王眞一學了道家氣功；並拜訪許多人士學了其他許多氣功功法。他還向金互、徐振寬先生學過儒家修身法。同時，他還從名師學了太極拳等內功掌。解放後，在北京一些高等院校，如北京工業學院、師範大學、師範學院、外語學院、礦業學院、中央戲劇學院、農業機械化學院、中國科學院、中央衛生進修學院教太極拳和氣功。所著《吳氏簡化太極拳》已出版。另外，所著《吳氏太極拳》一書的英文版已出版，中文版也即將出版。

二. 陳冠華：1924年生於江西省，現年61歲。1950年他畢業於清華大學電機系，1953年又畢業於北京俄專。作了四年俄文科技翻譯。從1956年起是電力工業部及其所屬部門的工程師。現是水電部科技情報研究所的高級工程師。

1946年他練過幾個月氣功。1963年重新學習了秦重三先生所教氣功後，堅持練功二十多年。1981年起，學習了王培生先生所教氣功。所寫已發表的氣功文章有：

1. "氣功主要是意功"，《氣功》1984年第3期。
2. "三田合一"，《氣功》1982年第2期。
3. "再談三田合一"，《氣功》1983年第1期。
4. "關於自發動功的幾點見解"，《氣功與科學》1984年第3期。
5. "Qigong: Mastering the Mind"，《中國日報》1984年12月31日。

三. Tony Rossi：1948年生，現年36歲。1974年畢業於美國加州漢博爾特大學地理系和教育系，獲文學士。1977年又畢業於該大學歷史系獲文學士。在澳大利亞教過6年歷史和地理。1980年起在中國教英語。現是中國科學院的英語教師。在唸大學時，Rossi先生學過4年印度瑜珈，最近又學習了本書所介紹的這套氣功功法。

前言

大家知道，氣功是一種健身治病的好方法。氣功在中國有五千多年的歷史。早在春秋戰國(公元前770——221年)時期的百家爭鳴中，氣功就已達到很高的程度。後來佛教又傳入了中國，更充實了氣功的內容。在幾千年的傳習中，氣功有許多發展。據說，中國由道、釋、儒、中醫、武術師及其他人士傳習的氣功有上千種。在中國，道家的氣功傳播最廣。

按道家的說法，練氣功可分爲五個階段，即煉谷化精，煉精化氣，煉氣化神，煉神還虛，煉虛合道。煉谷化精是築基階段。在這階段，得氣感開始出現，精液將增多。煉精化氣成後，氣能沿任(腹)督(背)二脈運行，即所謂小周天已通。煉氣化神成後，氣能沿全身主要經絡運行，即所謂大周天已通。煉神還虛成後，容易進入虛無態—— 一種覺得自己身體消失了的更高級的氣功態。

本書將介紹兩種築基功：松靜功和蛤蚌功，還將介紹一種煉精化氣功法，一種煉氣化神功法和三田合一功法，還將介紹進入虛無態的體驗和方法。這些功法簡單易行，見效快，可以循序漸進，逐步提高。青年人一般築基需一個月，煉成小周天需百日，煉成大周天需十八個月。年齡較大的和有病的人所需時間得更長些。只要每天堅持練功半小時至一小時，一般人都能達到這個程度。氣功並不神秘。

氣功主要是意功，即入靜、意守丹田、以意引氣、進入虛無態等意念功夫。(參看附錄一)。

本書有一節談“氣是什麼？”以幫助讀者瞭解中國氣功。

中國字“氣”，一般意指氣體，如空氣(air)。但有時氣的含義要廣泛得多，幾乎包括宇宙的一切，如有名的《正氣歌》中的“正氣”則包括日、星、山和河。中醫則認爲，人的生命有賴於元氣。現在一般將“元氣”譯爲“original (inborn) vital energy”。氣功之氣有時指呼吸的空氣，有時指人的元氣，有時指充斥宇宙的“氣”。但氣功尚有一種特殊而重要的氣，即練功一段時間之後，會感到意守處有發熱發脹等感覺，我們稱之爲“得氣感”。有時把這種氣叫做“眞氣”。這種得氣感隨着功夫的提高，會有所發展。例如，煉精化氣成後，此得氣感能循任督二脈運行，即所謂小周天；煉氣化神成後，此得氣感能循十二經和奇經八脈運行，即所謂大周天。也就是說，此得氣感會逐漸發展，最後達於全身。而這有利於恢復元氣，有利於健身治病。這種得氣感尚與所呼吸的空氣及充斥宇宙之氣有某種尚不清楚的聯系。例如，我們知道，得氣感是隨呼吸而起伏。什麼東西引起這種得氣感呢？現在尚不清楚。這裏將介紹一種設想。近些年研究發現，在練氣功入靜時，人腦會發出較特殊的腦電波，其頻率較低，波幅較大，有序性較高。從現代生理學，我們知道，人們手指會彎曲是因腦電波經神經系統送到手指處，該神經末梢放出某些化學物質，使有的肌肉伸，有的肌肉收縮而致該指彎曲。意守處的體溫要高1—3℃。因此，我們認爲入靜時發生的特殊腦電波經神經系統送到意守處，使該處微血管擴張，血流較充沛，使某些生理功能較旺盛，局部溫度略有上升，並伴生其他一些生理現象，因此，使練功者對該處有發熱發脹等感覺。

如上所述，得氣感是依賴意念的，但它在某種程度上又獨立於意念。**例如：**

1. 如果某人已有得氣感，則在小睡時，此種得氣感仍能保持。

2. 如對某穴位以前意守過並使之已通，則現在即使不意守該穴位，該處也易產生得氣感。

3. 有些穴位已“通”，即使你不意守該穴位，該處也可能有得氣感。

站、坐、臥都能練鬆靜功

姿勢：

1.站式（圖1）：兩脚分開與肩同寬，脚尖朝前，兩膝微曲，兩手自然下垂，手心向大腿。眼和嘴輕輕閉上。

2.坐式（圖2）：坐在一凳子上，兩脚平放地上，兩腿分開與肩同寬，曲膝成90°，大腿與軀幹垂直，兩掌輕放在大腿上，沉肩墮肘，下頷微收，含胸，眼和嘴輕閉。

3.臥式（圖3）：仰臥，頭在枕上，手臂放在身體兩側，手掌朝下，腿自然伸直，兩脚分開與肩同寬，脚尖朝上，眼和嘴輕閉。

姿勢擺好後，意念先想百會穴，旋即依次轉想肩井、膻中、中丹田、會陰、陰陵泉、三陰交和湧泉穴。然後，想大、二、三、四、小脚趾，並順此方向繞脚底板一周，意念再回到湧泉穴。最後，想着似乎兩脚各踏在一口井上，而湧泉穴下貼在井中水面上。當意想湧泉穴貼井下水面一定時間以後，思想不能集中時，可從脚底外側中間起，沿腿外側順次往上想陰陵泉、環跳、會陰、命門和

圖1.站式

圖2.坐式

中丹田；然後再從中丹田按上述路綫往下想，直至意想湧泉穴又貼在井下水面爲止。

此功可滋陰補腎，使濁氣下降、清氣上升，能治神經衰弱、氣管炎、高血壓、胸悶等病。

圖3. 臥式

這是一種築基功，這套功法大體分爲三階段，各以蛤蚌育肉、開懷、採氣作比喻，現分述於下：

1）育肉： 這是蛤蚌功的基本功。

站式（圖4）：兩脚分開同肩寬，脚尖朝前，兩膝微曲，鬆肩墮肘，兩手自然起來捧着肚子，眼和嘴輕輕閉上。兩中指尖隔着衣服扶在肚臍眼的邊緣上，手腕和肘都輕輕地（用意不用力）貼在帶脈上。然後想勞宮穴貼在帶脈上，開始時覺得似貼非貼，待到覺得已貼住時，就改想少海穴貼在帶脈上，開始時覺得似貼非貼，待到覺得貼住時，又回想勞宮穴貼帶脈，如此往復循環。這樣堅持的時間越長越好，但要以舒適爲度，要逐步延長時間。

這時覺得，似乎兩手捧着一個大球，兩脚踩着一個大球，頭頂也頂着一個大球，這三球相照，就是"三田合一"。

待到手捧的球似乎要突出時，就可轉入下一階段。

2）開懷：

兩中指尖離開肚臍眼，引導兩手伸向外向上，手指與肩井平時，似乎要觸着蛤蚌殼，但殼不開（圖5）。兩手又轉向下，以兩中指尖的中沖穴按摩氣沖穴。然後兩中指相繼按摩陰陵泉、三陰

圖4

圖5

交、懸鐘、陽陵泉和環跳穴。然後，兩手扶着後腰(圖6、7)，中指尖在命門穴，拇指朝下。以兩手心和命門為圓心各畫一圓，就形成圖8那樣的三個圓，這叫“三環套月”。三圓本是直立，要想着把三環擺成水平，這時身體後仰，像伸懶腰(但別用力)這就像蛤蚌已開懷。

這樣待一會兒，等到覺得兩脚心已入地，而頭頂百會穴貼地時，腰可伸直，像受力向後彎的籐條，當外力取消時，自然彈回來的樣子。這時，百會就會將湧泉的“水”引上來，這叫“龍頭引水”。

然後，鬆肩墮肘，兩手自然下垂，休息一會兒，就可轉入第三階段。

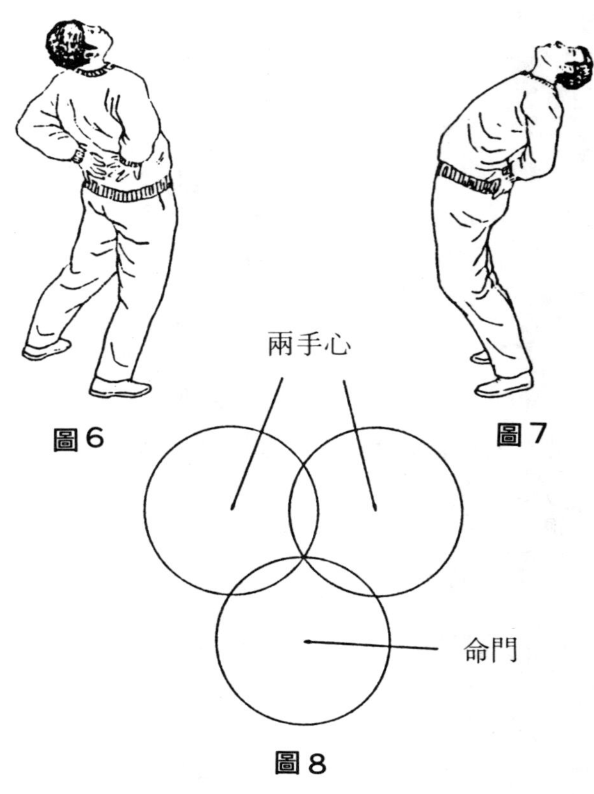

圖6

圖7

圖8

3）採氣：

兩手上舉，手心相對，肘微曲，掌心分開同眼寬。兩中指尖與眼同高時，中指相接，然後分開，使掌心分開同大脚趾尖的距離。似乎手指和脚趾中間各有一蚌殼，並且張開。然後，兩中指又回到中間相接後即張開，兩臂向左、右兩側斜上方伸出，掌心朝天（圖9）。這時脚跟離地，意念想着鼻子尖，盡吸天地之眞氣。然後，兩手指又回到中間相接，隨後鬆肩墮肘，兩手自然下落至腹前（圖10）；這時，意念想人中穴，將剛才吸得的氣下貫丹田。如此作7次，吸6口氣。

最好在農曆初一到初三，太陽出來時，面對太陽採氣，可得太陽的眞陰；在十五到十七日，晚上月亮升起時，面對月亮採氣，可得太陰的眞陽。

蛤蚌功最後還要作一會兒第一階段的"育肉"功，作爲收功。

練蛤蚌功可兼收"三田合一"和鬆靜功的效果。（"三田合一"下文將敍述）。

圖9

圖10

煉精化氣

精是人身之寶，應不使輕易排洩。將精煉成氣，就能使人輕靈、愉快，對健身治病大有好處。

煉精化氣要有一定氣功基礎。要先練鬆靜功、蛤蚌功等基本功，使陽氣充足後才能開始煉精化氣。精足，陽舉較頻，做氣功時帶脈得氣感較粗等現象是陽氣充足的象徵。自己可根據這些現象來判斷是否開始煉精化氣。

練功方法：

1. 吐三口和吸三口喉頭氣之後，就隨呼吸想肚臍和命門，吸時想命門，呼時想肚臍，呼吸要自然。練一定時間以後，就會感到呼氣時，氣從中丹田(肚臍內)經會陰直貫湧泉；吸時氣從湧泉經會陰回至命門。這時後三關中的長强穴自然就會通，因吸氣收腹尾閭前移時，氣會從會陰到長强。
2. 在此基礎上，就可通後三關的其它兩關，即夾脊和玉枕。夾脊在背上大椎下三寸，玉枕在腦後風府穴下的窩窩處。通夾脊的方法是：呼時想肚臍，吸時想夾脊，初起時會感到夾脊發木，然後感到發脹發熱，再後感到氣從命門直貫夾脊，而且這種得氣感會越來越强，越來越粗，待夾脊處的得氣感達到一手掌寬時，夾脊就通了。然後就可通玉枕，待玉枕處得氣感達一手掌寬時，玉枕就通了。
3. 在後三關已通的基礎上，當氣至玉枕時，就可意想將眼向上向後視，然後向前視，將氣從玉枕迎至頭頂百會穴。停一會兒，氣會行至百會和腦門的中間。那時頭頂會感到清涼濕潤，全身感到很舒服。應力求較長期保持這種舒服感，這就是煉精化氣已成。這時不應有任何雜念。
4. 當上述舒服感保持不住時，氣會下降。氣下降時，應聽其自然，不要用意引導，否則可能走偏或阻滯。一般氣在臉部分三路(鼻和兩眼)下降，集中在人中。那時可將舐住上顎的舌放平，氣就會下來，這叫搭鵲橋，使任督二脈接通。然後氣會從任脈或冲脈下降到中丹田，這就完成了一次小周天。

5. 按上述方法繼續做小周天，但一般每次作功時，小周天不要超過九次。最後氣歸丹田收功。

注意事項：

立、坐、臥時都可煉化氣。但臥時枕頭應高些，氣在頭頂不要停留。

練功時應力求沒有雜念，但不要用意過緊。氣上頭頂後，不要用意想氣停留處的穴位，否則可能上火。而要注意保持舒服感，對氣應不忘不助，聽其自然。

煉精化氣一般百日可成，但要注意循序漸進，穩步前進，待前一步有一定效應後再作下一步。這樣只有好處，不會出毛病。否則，欲速則不達，還可能出毛病。

在煉精化氣已成的基礎上，就能煉氣化神。此功練成後，可使氣通全身十二經和奇經八脈，氣隨意行，意到氣到，能使人精神爽，身輕靈，百病除。

練功方法：

1. 舌在口內攪三次，吞津液時，氣隨津液下直至恥骨，意也至恥骨。
2. 恥骨得氣後，意念轉至大脚趾尖。
3. 大脚趾得氣後，一鬆大脚趾，意轉想脚跟，然後相繼想委中、環跳和會陰。
4. 氣從會陰過肛門至長强後，意想夾脊。
5. 夾脊得氣後，轉想腋下極泉、手中指尖的中冲、肩井、又回至夾脊。
6. 然後想玉枕。玉枕得氣後，想耳後根，然後想耳上方繞耳轉一至三週，回到玉枕。
7. 玉枕得氣較粗後，用眼迎氣至百會，氣在頭頂不停，沿面部直下人中，經舌轉至任脈。這就完成了一輪大周天。
8. 每三輪大周天攪舌三次(將津液嚥下)，共作九輪，所以此法又叫“九轉還魂丹”。
9. 收功時，引氣回中丹田。

注意事項：

1. 此功站、坐、臥都能練。姿勢同鬆靜功。
2. 不管呼吸，眼自然閉上。
3. 前穴得氣後再想下一穴，別操之過急。
4. 初練時，只想所述穴位，不想經脈，練到一定時候，經脈自通。
5. 練功時，如出現各種幻景及其它走火入魔現象，應不聞不問，不爲所動。
6. 驚功後，可用大手指尖按無名指指根，並按摩手背內外側，自可緩解。
7. 煉氣化神成功後，可用意引氣至阿是穴(病痛處)，治療自己的疾病。
8. 練功時，如出現覺得自己似有似無的恍惚狀况，並有特別的舒服感，應力求保持這種狀况，這就是煉神化虛。

中國道、釋、儒、中醫、武術師所傳習的氣功大都追求同一目標，即進入虛無態。簡單地說，各家氣功通虛無。進入虛無態的情況和感覺，因人因時而有所不同。

虛無態對治病健身甚爲有益。進入虛無態之前要引氣去治病，而進入虛無態之後，病會自己出來，其疼痛情況和發病時相似。病出來以後，可意守疼痛處5——10分種。輕病和新病，如較輕的感冒，一次就能痊癒；而老病和較重的病，要多次才能好。

如何才能進入虛無態呢？第一，要求思想安靜、無所掛慮，精神和身體都放鬆。第二，要求環境安靜。第三，大周天已通，即進入全身得氣的狀態。那時，意念要減輕，什麼都別想。有時，總想進入虛無，反而不能進入，而不想時倒能進入。有時，處於一種似睡非睡的狀態倒易進入虛無態。古人說："有意都是假，無意方是眞"，當是講這時的情景。一般仰臥做氣功，較易進入虛無態，而站時可回想進入虛無態時的感覺，也可有助於進入虛無態。

進入虛無態有什麼現象呢？第一個現象，就是進入虛無態的一會兒時間，眼前出現一片白光，額前有一鈕扣大的帶色小光點。第二個現象，就是感到自己的身體消失了。第三個現象，就是人體的自我調節機能提高了，如延長練功時間仍能保持舌下生津，長期不排尿，不放屁等現象。第四個現象，就是體表的電阻似乎降低了。

此外，尚需指出一種很重要的現象：有一個人原來長期練站樁功，有一段時間，他爲了更多進入虛無態，只有仰臥練功，而不煉站樁功；這時，他的腿力就有所減弱。後來，他改練睡功又練站樁功，他的腿力又恢復了。這個例子說明，我們必需把進入虛無態和其他練習結合起來，才能達到"性命雙修"的目的。

三田合一

這是老道士王眞一傳習的一種功法。三田合一就是用意念把上、中、下三個丹田擺在一條直綫上。做到三田合一時，自己感到很舒服，似乎忘掉一切，大、小周天自然通，很容易消除疲勞，不管再疲勞，只要三田合一15分鐘，就能完全消除。直立、平臥、斜躺、打太極拳和騎自行車時都能作三田合一，不必作預備功和收功。

三田合一的具體作法如下：

1. 想上丹田後，立即轉想下丹田。
2. 待下丹田放正而有發熱發脹等得氣感時，就想中丹田，想把中丹田放在上、下丹田的聯綫上，使三個丹田成一線。這時，上、中、下三個丹田好像是三個球，中丹田這個球要很小心才能穩定放在上、下兩球中間，一不小心就會滑出去。
3. 三田眞合一時，就會產生一種特殊的快感。應力求保持這種舒服感，保持的時間越長越好，可使人返本還原，健身治病。這時要專心注意這種舒服感，不要有雜念。

主要注意事項

1. 要有信心、決心和恆心。
2. 要力求靜、鬆。
3. 要順其自然求自然，對練功中出現的各種反應漠然視之，不有意追求，出現時也不奇怪，不驚恐或過份喜悅，總之要不求有功，但求無"過"，求不出毛病。
4. 初學者意念應多在四肢(如手心、脚掌等)，就可不出毛病。
5. 初學者最好不管呼吸，即採取自然呼吸。
6. 別輕易將氣引上頭部，否則可能上火，可能引起血熱、頭髮早白。有的患者，如偏頭痛患者，採用意守阿是穴療法必須引氣上頭時，需增加意守湧泉穴和命門穴，以便降火。練功正確時，口內不斷生津，上火時，則口乾舌枯。有時意守湧泉過多，也會口乾舌枯，那時，應意守命門，使水引上來。掌握火候是練氣功始終要注意的一個重要問題。
7. 有些功法，如鬆靜功、蛤蚌功第一階段，練功時間越長越好，但不能操之過急。要逐漸延長，以舒適不累爲度。練功時，感到口乾舌枯，如非雜念過多，就可能是練功過長、太累所致，那時，就應收功。
8. 人們精液非常寶貴，不可輕易洩放。例如，夢遺時感到精液要外洩時，可立即像忍大便那樣忍住，並用意將精液引回。然後用意引過後三關(長强、夾脊和玉枕三穴)到頭頂百會穴。這也叫"煉精化氣"。
9. 收功時，應引氣回中丹田。
10. 收功後，應進行適當的按摩。(參閱新世界出版社出版的《中國傳統的健身法》一書)。

氣功主要是意功*

把氣功譯成英語的"a system of breathing exercises"(《中國日報》1984年10月19日)可能使外國人產生誤解。

我練功已二十多年。氣功對健身長壽大有好處，氣功治好了我許多疾病；如脂肪肝、關節炎、鼻炎、胃痛和偏頭痛。我練了十多種氣功，其中大部分功法是不管呼吸，即保持自然呼吸。有的功法要求調息，但仍以調心爲主。因此，我寫了一篇文章，題爲《氣功主要是意功》。該文已發表於《氣功》雜誌1981年第4期。

據說中國由道、釋、儒、武術師、中醫和其他人士傳習的氣功有上千種。在這許多氣功中，有沒有共同點呢？我認爲，對大多數氣功來說，其共同點是：靜鬆自然。靜即入靜，除練功要點外，什麼也別想。鬆即保持身心放鬆。"自然"即要遵循自然規律，不緊張。

對於大多數高級氣功，還有另一個共同點，這就是：進入"虛無態"。人們進入"虛無態"時，感到自己的身體似乎沒有了。進入"虛無態"對健身長壽甚爲有益。在上述這些共同點中，意功是最重要的。氣功中的調息是次要的，不是關鍵。

北京陳冠華

***注：** 本文引自《中國日報》1984年12月31日

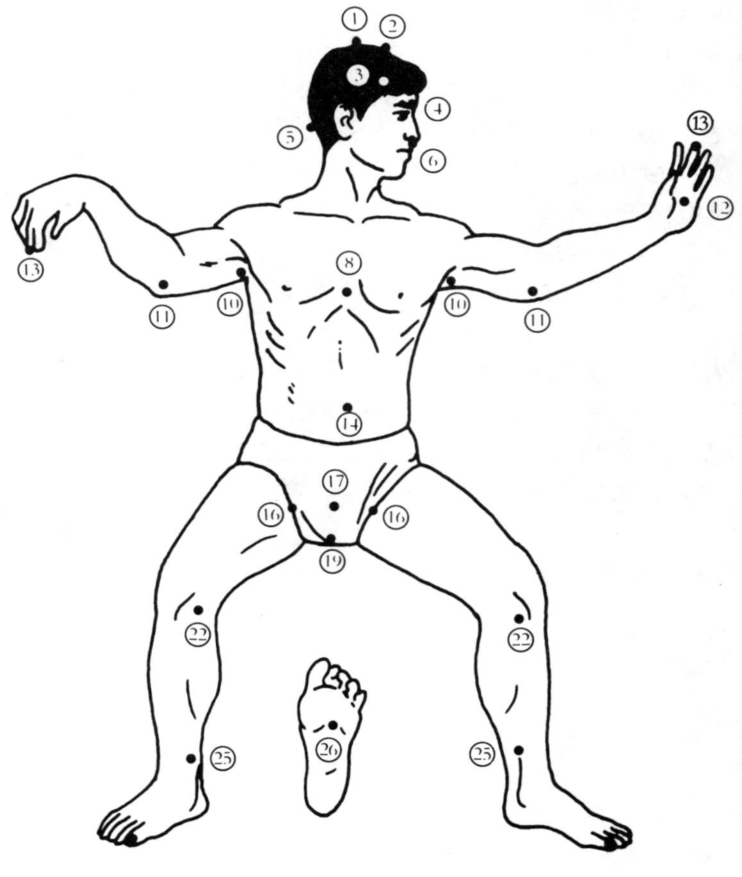
1
2
3
4
5
6
8
10
10
11
11
12
13
13
14
16
16
17
19
22
22
25
25
26

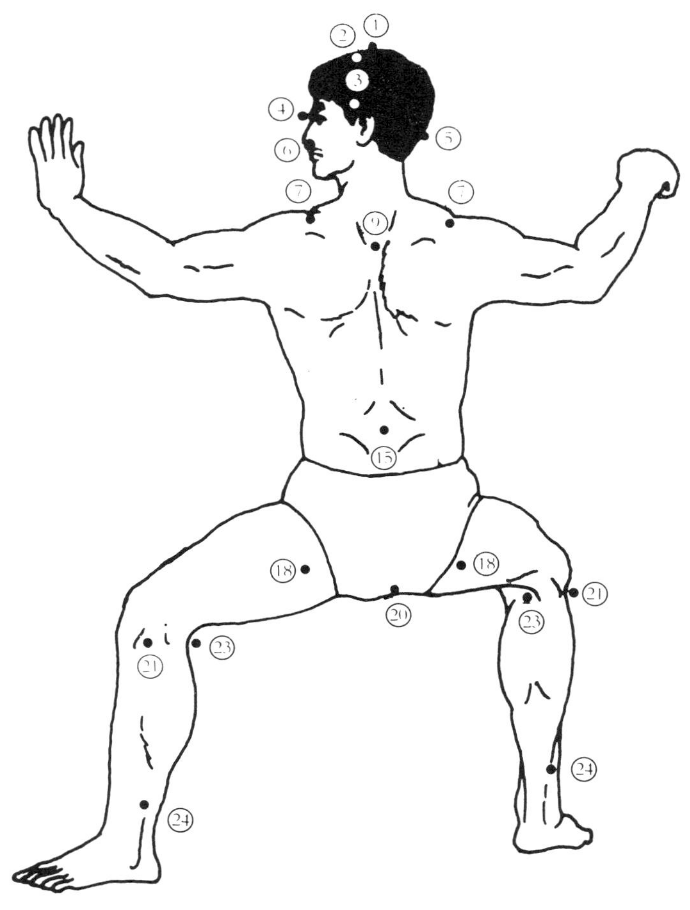

1. 百會　2. 腦門　3. 上丹田　4. 玄關　5. 玉枕　6. 人中　7. 肩井
8. 膻中　9. 夾脊　10. 極泉　11. 少海　12. 勞宮　13. 中沖
14. 中丹田　15. 命門　16. 氣沖　17. 恥骨　18. 環跳
19. 下丹田(會陰)　20. 長强　21. 陽陵泉　22. 陰陵泉　23. 委中
24. 懸鐘　25. 三陰交　26. 湧泉

有關穴位部位表

編號	穴 名	部 位
1	百 會	頭頂窩窩處。
2	腦 門	相當於嬰孩腦骨未長成處。
3	上丹田	兩眉間的玄關穴往後1寸和腦門下1寸的腦內。
4	玄 關	兩眉間。
5	玉 枕	腦後髮際正中上約1寸，相當枕骨粗隆下的窩窩處。
6	人 中	上嘴唇中上方的人中溝中。
7	肩 井	兩手在胸前交叉伸掌握對側肩，大拇指貼頸時，中指尖處就是肩井穴。
8	膻 中	心窩處。
9	夾 脊	第七頸椎棘穴下的大椎穴往下3寸處。
10	極 泉	在腋窩。
11	少 海	屈肘，肘横紋尺側頭。
12	勞 宮	在手掌中心。
13	中 冲	中指尖中央。
14	中丹田	肚臍內離肚臍3／10，離背脊命門7／10處。
15	命 門	背脊上與肚臍相對處。
16	氣 冲	在大腿與軀幹間横紋上，横紋中點偏下1寸。
17	恥 骨	
18	環 跳	股骨大轉子後方的窩窩處。
19	下丹田	即會陰穴。男子爲陰囊與肛門之間處。女子爲大陰唇後聯合與肛門之間處。
20	長 强	尾骨尖下五分處。
21	陽陵泉	屈膝，小腿外側，腓骨小頭前下緣小窩處。

編號	穴名	部位
22	陰陵泉	屈膝，脛骨內髁下緣窩窩處。
23	委中	膕橫紋中央(膝後)。
24	懸鐘	又名絕骨。外踝尖上3寸，腓骨後緣。
26	湧泉	前腳掌心，蹺足時窩窩處。

注：1寸等於中指中節兩橫紋間的距離。

例一：治好脂肪肝的實例：

陳冠華，男，現年61歲，水電部科技情報研究所高級工程師。

1981年練這套氣功以前，他雖已練氣功十多年，但小周天似通非通，對大周天不敢輕試，全身得氣的狀態只偶而出現。他自1981年練這套功法後，大、小周天很快就通了，而且較常能進入較高級的氣功態——虛無態。隨着功法的提高，他的身體大有好轉。他肝區疼痛二十多年來時隱時現，1980年經超聲波檢查，診斷爲脂肪肝，吃了100多劑中藥，未能治好，西醫更表示無法治好。而他練這套氣功，把脂肪肝治好了。1984年超聲波檢查結果已看不出異常症狀，自覺肝區疼痛也消失了。而1981——1984年期間，他並未採取氣功以外的任何其他治療脂肪肝的措施。

練這套功法，不易出毛病，而且可按不同情況調整功法，糾正偏差。例如，陳冠華在過去練氣功時，意守頭部較多，易上火，眼易花，髮早白；而練這套功法後，上火現象有所緩解，眼花較少了，身體更健康了。另外，這套功法重調心，不重調息。陳冠華過去練過一套重調息的氣功，有時調息不當，引起胸脅痛等毛病；而練這套功法，則不會產生這種毛病。

另外，這套功法由築基，經煉精化氣、煉氣化神，到煉神還虛，每步都有自己可以掌握的標準和現象，利於練功者由淺到深，逐步提高，穩步前進。

例二：練"三田合一"消除疲勞的實例。

張占魁，在湖北省黃陂縣羅漢鄉春建小學工作。他練"三田合一"後，體會總結這一功法有如下三個優點：

1. 容易入靜　練此功法時不象其它功法那樣只意守某一部位。意守比較單調，不易入靜。"三田合一"要求意守上、中、下三個丹田，並且使上、中、下三個丹田貫穿在一條直線上，這樣就使意念有所注引，能使氣血有規則地運行，不致氣血亂竄，出現偏差；有利於疏通經絡；使人情緒較快得到安定，雜念較快消除，容易進入氣功狀態。

2. 花時間短　以前他練過太極氣功，一天三次，花費時間兩小時左右；由於功法複雜，練功時對環境要求較高，往往受到客觀條件的限制，“驚功”經常發生。練“三田合一”功法無需做預備和收功，只要有短暫的休息時間都可以練習，即使中途受人干擾，對練功者也無副作用。他熟練後一般練功15分鐘就能達到氣功狀態。

3. 功效顯著　由於練“三田合一”入靜快，容易進入氣功狀態，因此也就易於取得祛病健身的效果。練功時口中津液涓涓不斷，練功後食欲旺盛，睡眠酣甜，精力相當充沛。以前，他工作到深夜，第二天就感到精神不振，工作效率下降。現在，他無論工作到什麼時候，甚至通宵，只要工作結束時練功15—30分鐘，第二天照常工作，毫無倦意。他在繁重的體力勞動以後練“三田合一”，功效也同樣顯著。農村大忙季節，他往往一天從事重體力勞動十多小時，練功後即能消除疲勞。

（引自《氣功》1983年第5期）

例三：練“三田合一”，防止和糾正偏差的實例。

蘇五，在湖北竹山縣官渡中學工作。他練紅砂手將近一年後，能氣達指掌，雙手掌力很大；但是，在一階段內，他練功很難入靜，氣不能引入中丹田，只在腹內亂竄。無論採用貫氣法或其他方法，都未能生效。他學會“三田合一”後，在每次練功前，先練“三田合一”5——10分鐘，不到3天，氣血亂竄的毛病就消除了。同時，在練功中，還發現此法不僅能防偏差，還能幫助入靜、全身放鬆和消除失眠症。

（引自《氣功》1984年第2期）

例四：治好癔病、胃病和冠心病的實例。

文昇蘭，女，現年48歲，在地質礦產部會議樓（即招待所）工作。

1966年以前，她渾身疼痛了幾年，但查不出原因。1966年3月，她病情加重，哭鬧不止，喜怒無常，經北醫三院診斷爲癔病。西醫和中醫治療多年，均未治好；後又發生冠心病，血壓升高，心絞痛時而出現；再加上老胃病復發，使她幾度病危，送醫院搶救。她有時突然暈倒，脈搏微弱。有時心跳間歇頻繁。那時，她身體極度虛弱。夏天還要穿一條厚棉褲和二條毛褲和棉鞋，而且同房屋的人都不能搧扇子。她自己更不能搧扇子，否則就感到骨頭痛。那時，她稍受驚嚇，兩腿就發麻，不能行走。

1982年以後，她學練了王培生老師所教氣功和37式太極拳(參閱王培生、曾維祺著《吳氏太極拳》)，堅持鍛練，病情便日見好轉，身體逐漸康復。現在，她的癔病已治好，心絞痛已久未出現，而四十年的老胃病也不見再犯了。同時，她原患的關節炎、盆腔炎、嚴重便秘和腹部腫脹等毛病也都治好了。身體健康了，夏天不必穿棉褲、毛褲和棉鞋，熱時，自己能搧扇子。她說：「過去我是重病人。氣功和太極拳救了我。我是個從死神手中逃脫出來的人。」

例五：治療高血壓，腎炎和痔瘡的實例。

徐文明，男，現年60歲，北京電車公司司機。

他患高血壓，腎炎、痔瘡等多種疾病。血壓高達190／120毫米汞柱。驗尿結果爲：尿蛋白兩個加號；白血球0.3—0.5；紅血球0.5—1.0。痔瘡術後收斂不好，一上火就有腫包。

從1983年6月，他練了王培生老師所教氣功和37式太極拳後，每天早晨練一個半小時，取得了顯著的療效。現在，他的血壓已下降到150／100毫米汞柱；驗尿結果只有一個加號，白血球0.1，紅血球0.3，說明腎炎已明顯減輕。他的痔瘡也徹底治愈。同時，他脾的毛病也好了。能吃能睡，走路輕便；能較長時間工作而不疲勞，已一年多沒上醫院看過病。而且脾氣也變好了。

例六：治好肝炎的實例。

張錫修，男，現年50歲，在北京核儀器廠工作。

他於1983年患肝炎，轉氨酶高達495(正常爲160以下)。那時，除了適當休息和吃些保肝藥物外，他練了王培生老師所教鬆靜功和37式太極拳；練功和打拳時，他的意念多放在無名指尖。一個月後復查，他的轉氨酶降到66，其它肝功能指標也正常。大夫當時也感到驚奇，說：「好的眞快！」

例七：治好冠心病和便秘的實例。

張淑筠，女，現年61歲，北京外國語學院幹部。

她原患冠心病，時有期前收縮和心絞痛。另外，她便秘較嚴重。她從1981年練王培生老師所教這套氣功和37式太極拳後，這兩種病都逐漸好轉。現在，她期前收縮和心絞痛已很久不發生，大便也正常了。

例八：治好健忘症和虛胖的實例。

彭文章，男，現年53歲，地質礦產部辦公廳秘書處秘書。

他原患健忘症，開會作記錄時，熟人的名字也記不下來，文件也不能看，而且睡不好，性急，易發火(過去無此現象)。他從1984年上半年學練王培生老師所教氣功和37式太極拳後，療效很好。現在，他能吃能睡，記憶力恢復正常，不但能做記錄和看文件，還能寫文章。同時，他原有的虛胖現象也已消失，變得更結實，走路也更利索。

例九：返老還童的實例。

謝善初，男，74歲，原是北京商人，現居北京西城區東養馬房30號。他原來身體很虛弱，走路老態龍鐘。但從1983年起，學練王培生老師所教氣功和37式太極拳後，變得年青了。現在，他走路像個小伙子。